W9-BLA-929

FAST FAMILIES: Racing Together Through Life

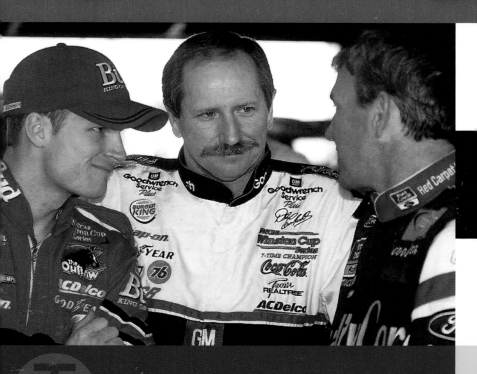

T RADITION BOOKS™
EXCELSIOR, MINNESOTA

BY TED BROCK

Published by **Tradition Books**™ and distributed to the
school and library market by **The Child's World**®
P.O. Box 326
Chanhassen, MN 55317-0326
800/599-READ
http://www.childsworld.com

Photo Credits
Cover and title page: AP/Wide World
Allsport: 10, 15 (Adam Pretty); 28 (Chris Stanford)
AP/Wide World: 5, 7, 11, 14, 16, 25, 26
Sports Gallery: 8, 9 (Tom Riles); 13, 20 top, 27 (Al Messerschmidt); 17, 18,
  20 bottom, 21 left, 22, 23 (Brian Spurlock); 19, 21 right, 29 (Joe Robbins)

Book production by Shoreline Publishing Group, LLC
Art direction and design by The Design Lab

Library of Congress Cataloging-in-Publication Data

Brock, Ted.
  Fast families : racing together through life / by Ted Brock.
    p. cm. — (The world of NASCAR series)
Summary: Describes the history and achievements of notable families involved in stock car
racing, including the Frances, the Pettys, and the Elliotts. Includes bibliographical references
and index.
  ISBN 1-59187-005-4   38888000014658
  1. Automobile racing drivers—United States—Biography—Juvenile literature. 2. NASCAR
(Association)—History—Juvenile literature. 3. Automobile racing drivers—United States—
Family relationships—Juvenile literature. [1. Automobile racing drivers. 2. NASCAR
(Association)—History. 3. Stock car racing—History.] I. Title. II. Series.
  GV1032.A1 B76 2002
  796.72'092'2—dc21   2002004644

Printed in the United States of America.

FAST FAMILIES

Table of Contents

INTRODUCTION

A Family Affair

W hen fans and drivers talk about "the NASCAR family,"
they're not just using an expression. Families are as
much a part of stock car racing's highest level as
gasoline and tires.

For instance, no other professional sport is family owned.
There are football, basketball, baseball, and hockey teams
owned by families. NASCAR is the only sports organization
owned by a family, however. Bill France and Bill France Jr.
have run the organization since it began in 1948. A third
generation of Frances is ready to take over.

The Frances came from Minnesota and moved to
Daytona, Florida. They soon turned that seaside town into
the capital of stock car racing. First they founded NASCAR to
organize the popular sport of stock car racing. Then, in 1959,

they built the famous Daytona International Speedway.

During NASCAR's history, there have been all kinds of family combinations on and off the track. More than a dozen father-and-son pairs have raced. Several pairs (and even trios) of brothers have battled against each other on the track. At one point, fans watched as three brothers and their sister all climbed into cars. Bob, Fonty, Ted, and Ethel Flock all raced stock cars.

The number of driving families in NASCAR is impressive. Each family's story adds its special flavor to the history of stock car racing. The tradition is passed down from generation to generation. Stock car racing is truly a family affair.

Dale Earnhardt, father of a racer, shakes hands with NASCAR chairman Bill France Jr., son of the series founder.

The King and His Court

The Pettys are the "royal" family of stock car racing. Four generations of Pettys have come out of North Carolina to become top racing stars. Lee, Richard, Kyle, and Adam Petty together formed the most successful family in stock car racing history. In fact, they might also be the greatest sports family of all time.

Lee Petty was a **NASCAR** pioneer and one of the top racers of his time. He started out racing stock cars on short dirt tracks in the South. Lee was one of the first drivers to join NASCAR when it was formed. He went on to win 54 races before he stopped driving. Among his career highlights was a victory in the first Daytona 500 in 1959. He also won three NASCAR championships.

Watching all of Lee's success was his son, Richard. The

young man who would grow up to be called "the King"
learned about racing in his father's garage. He started racing
against his dad as soon as he turned 21. Richard won his first
race in 1960. He didn't stop until more than 30 years and 200
victories later. His career win total is almost twice as many as
any other driver.

Also watching was Richard's brother Maurice. He drove
for a while, but soon turned his attention to the garage.
Maurice became the sport's top engine builder. His work
under the hood of their number 43 car helped make his
brother a champion.

Maurice, Lee, and Richard Petty combined their
talents to form the first great NASCAR family.

Richard won the Daytona 500 seven times. He won seven season championships. His reign as "the King" hit it big in 1964 when he won his first Daytona 500. In 1967, the King had his greatest success. With Maurice fine-tuning the Chrysler engine, Richard sped to 27 victories. His total smashed the old single-season record of 18. Even more amazing was Richard's mark of 10 consecutive victories. No driver has come close to equaling that number.

Even though Richard retired in 1992, the Petty legacy continued. By then, Richard's son Kyle had been racing for

Richard Petty drove his famous number 43 car to an all-time record 200 NASCAR wins.

13 years. Kyle won the first stock car race he entered at age 18 in 1979. His dad teased him after the race. "You know what it's like to win, son. Now all you got to do is learn how to drive."

In 1986, Kyle became the first grandson of a NASCAR driver to win a **Winston Cup** event. In 1992 and 1993, he ranked fifth in the Winston Cup point standings . . . his highest finish.

The tradition continued when Adam Petty, Kyle's son, joined the stock car circuit. He began at a lower level and tried to work his way up to the top NASCAR races. His dream came true when he raced in an event in Texas in 2000.

Richard's son Kyle carried on the family tradition of winning. His dad is shown here in his trademark cowboy hat.

"We have a cool relationship," Adam said about his dad. "It's a father-and-son relationship Monday to Wednesday. Then from Wednesday to Sunday we're more brothers or best friends than we are anything."

Sadly, Adam was killed in a crash during a practice run in May 2000. It was only a month after Lee Petty had died at age 86. Richard continued to be active in the sport as a team owner. Kyle continues racing, keeping the Petty name a part of NASCAR, just like it's been since the beginning.

Adam Petty followed his grandfather and father to the track, but his career ended tragically.

THE ALLISONS

The story of another famous NASCAR family is a sad one. Bobby Allison (right) was one of the top drivers of the 1970s and 1980s. He often challenged Richard Petty on the track and in the NASCAR points race. Bobby won 85 races in his career, including three Daytona 500s. In his 1988 Daytona victory, he held off his son Davey on the final lap. Bobby also was the 1983 NASCAR champion, while finishing second in the standings five times.

Bobby's brother Donnie was the 1967 NASCAR Rookie of the Year. He was not as successful as Bobby in NASCAR. He was, however, more versatile. He raced just about every kind of car on tracks around the world. His most memorable NASCAR moment came in 1979. Cale Yarborough and Donnie bumped each other in the Daytona 500. After the race, Cale and Bobby had a fistfight on pit row.

Bobby's two sons, Davey and Clifford, both followed their dad and uncle into racing. Davey won 19 Winston Cup races, including the Daytona 500 in 1992. Sadly, Clifford died in a crash in 1992. Davey was killed the next year in a helicopter accident at Talladega Speedway.

11

CHAPTER TWO

In the Car and in the Shop

T he driver known as "Awesome Bill from Dawsonville" has been named NASCAR's most popular driver 15 times. Dawsonville, Georgia, native Bill Elliott has been a fan favorite and a winner from his first years on the track.

He has had a lot of help from his family along the way. Bill and his brother Ernie have become one of the sport's most successful and veteran teams. Bill does the driving, while Ernie is a key part of the racing team.

No driver can succeed without help behind the scenes. It takes more than 20 people to service the car during a race, including the **pit crew.** Dozens more help in the team office, at the garage, and while the team travels. The Elliott family makes their team one of the most family oriented on the circuit. Ernie has built all of Bill's engines, beginning when Bill drove a Ford car. Today, the duo works with owner Ray Evernham on Dodge cars.

That togetherness has taken the Elliotts to Victory Lane 41 times since they joined the Winston Cup circuit full time in 1983. Prior to that, they raced on short tracks in their home state.

The 2002 season was the Elliott brothers' 27th Winston Cup campaign. With more than 600 races under their belt, they're a legendary fixture on the circuit. Bill is one of only seven drivers with more than $20 million in career earnings. His only season championship came in 1988. He also finished in the top four in points in seven other years. His biggest wins came in the 1985 and 1987 Daytona 500.

In 1985, Bill earned another nickname. By winning three important 500-mile (800 kilometer) races,

Whether he's called "Awesome Bill from Dawsonville" or "Million Dollar Bill," Bill Elliott is always a winner.

he earned a bonus of $1 million. After that, he was known as "Million Dollar Bill."

In 1987, Ernie's engine and Bill's driving skill combined to set a new record. While qualifying for the Winston 500 in North Carolina, Bill's car reached an all-time best 212.809 miles per hour (342.41 kilometers per hour).

The two brothers used their talents for driving and engineering to reach the top. Their determination to succeed helped them stay on top. "Winning is very satisfying," Ernie

For winning the 1987 Daytona 500, Bill got two kisses, a T-shirt, and a very big pile of money.

says. "That's what I get paid for. But winning just makes us work that much harder."

Bill is a winner off the track, too. Along with his awards for popularity, he has earned honors for his charity. Bill has been named NASCAR's Man of the Year for his community work. He also works hard to raise money to fight cancer. Bill and Ernie's nephew Casey died of the disease at age 21. Bill also regularly meets with children through the Make-A-Wish Foundation.

Driving in 2002 in a new Dodge Intrepid, Bill continues to be a big factor in every NASCAR race.

THE JARRETTS

Dale Jarrett (in the car, above) has had a great NASCAR career. He won four races in 2001 to bring his career total to 28. He was the Winston Cup champion in 1999. He has also won three Daytona 500s, one of only four drivers to reach that total. Dale was the only driver to finish in the top four in the Winston Cup standings each year from 1996 to 1999.

For all of his success, however, he's still chasing his dad. Ned Jarrett (with microphone, above) was a two-time NASCAR champion, in 1961 and 1965. Before retiring in 1966 at age 35, Ned won 50 series races. That places him tenth all-time. He also won two championships at lower levels of stock car racing. The driver known as "Gentleman Ned" entered the Motorsports Hall of Fame in 1972.

Now there are two Jarretts chasing Grandpa Ned's record. Dale's son Jason raced in the Busch circuit, one level below NASCAR. In 1998, he and Dale raced together at Charlotte. Dale finished one place ahead of his son.

"It was almost like a dream," Jason said about racing against his dad.

"It was a lot more fun than I thought it would be!" Dale said after the race.

CHAPTER THREE

Brotherly Love

NASCAR drivers battle nose to nose at high speeds in important races. They are known for their hard-charging style. They don't let anything get in their way. In the case of the Labontes, that means not even letting a brother get ahead of you.

Bobby and Terry Labonte are the only brothers in their sport who both have won Winston Cup

Terry Labonte has twice been the Winston Cup champion.

championships. Terry won in 1984 and 1996. Bobby matched his older brother with a championship in 2000.

The brothers grew up around race cars in Corpus Christi, Texas. From the start, they were a team. In 1978, Terry was the first of the pair to earn a ride on the Winston Cup circuit, NASCAR's highest. Terry notched his first win in 1980. Soon he began a record streak of entering 655 races in a row.

Only six years later, Terry became the first of the brothers to win the season championship. Brother Bobby was a member of Terry's pit crew during that 1984 year. The pair celebrated together like only brothers can.

Bobby wanted to join his brother on the track, however. He started out in the Busch Series, one level below the

Bobby Labonte followed his brother to the top of the Winston Cup rankings in 2000.

Winston Cup races. Bobby was the Busch champion in 1991 in only his second full-time season. He nearly won it again in 1992. In 1993, the brothers saw their dream come true when Bobby graduated to Winston Cup racing.

Soon, he was battling Terry for position on the track and in Victory Lane. Bobby got his first race victory in 1995, in the Coca-Cola 600 at Charlotte. He has won at least one race every year since then.

The two brothers

One of Bobby's biggest wins came in the 2001 Brickyard 400.

shared a special moment in the last race of the 1996 season, the Napa 500 in Atlanta. Bobby, seven years younger, won the race. Terry finished fifth. However, that gave him enough points to nail down his second Winston Cup title.

Bobby and Terry drove a **victory lap** side-by-side, with Terry in tears behind the wheel. Later he called it "the most memorable day I've ever had in racing, without a doubt. Nothing else comes close to that." That's brotherly love, for sure.

Familiar sights on any NASCAR track are the speeding cars driven by the Labonte boys—Bobby (top) and Terry.

THE WALLACES

Rusty Wallace and his brothers Mike and Kenny grew up in St. Louis, Missouri. Their father Russ regularly won stock car races held on local dirt and asphalt tracks. He built the cars in the family's backyard. His boys picked up his aggressive, competitive nature.

Years later, they turned that love of cars and that competitive spirit into NASCAR victory. Rusty has had most of the trio's success. He was the Rookie of the Year in 1984 and won the series championship in 1989. He won at least one race every season from 1986 through 2001.

Former Busch series driver Mike Wallace came along next to join Rusty. He has competed in more than 70 races since 1991. His best finish came in 2001, when he was second in a race in Phoenix.

The youngest brother is Kenny. He worked his way up to Winston Cup racing by winning eight races in the Busch series. In 1993, he was third in the voting for Winston Cup Rookie of the Year. He has started more than 260 races in 11 NASCAR seasons.

A highlight of the brothers' career came in 1991. The trio raced in the 500-mile (805-kilometer) event at Phoenix. They were the first set of three brothers in a NASCAR race since the Flocks in 1961.

Kenny Wallace (left) joined brother Rusty (center) and Mike as a rare trio of siblings in NASCAR.

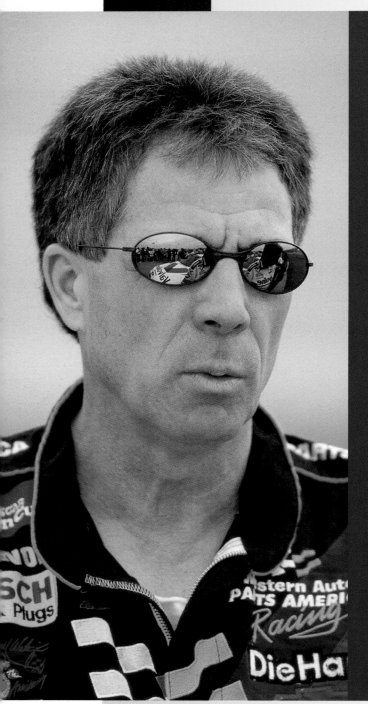

THE WALTRIPS

Darrell Waltrip (left) had many successful days on the race track. He won three Winston Cup championships (1981, 1982, and 1985). He won the 1989 Daytona 500. Fans twice voted him the Most Popular Driver.

Some of his greatest thrills, however, came when racing with and against his younger brother, Michael. Michael joined Darrell on the Winston Cup circuit in 1985. Though he was a good driver, he started more than 460 races without earning a victory.

In 2001, Michael joined the race team run by the legendary Dale Earnhardt. Michael took to the track for the Daytona 500 in his new number 15 car. The Daytona race is the most important event each year on the NASCAR circuit. Up in the press box, Darrell watched his brother line up in the starting grid. Darrell had retired and was working for the television network.

Five hundred miles later, Michael Waltrip was a winner for the first time in his career. On TV, older brother Darrell was proud. "Me and my brother have just won the Daytona 500!" he shouted.

Michael Waltrip has earned more than $10 million in prize money since joining Darrell in NASCAR in 1985.

C H A P T E R   F O U R

Carrying the Torch

Perhaps no racer today means more to the "NASCAR family" than Dale Earnhardt Jr. Certainly few sons have had greater fathers to live up to. Dale Earnhardt Sr. had one of the greatest careers in NASCAR history. "Junior" is just starting out, but he's gotten off on the right foot.

Dale the father joined the Winston Cup circuit full time in 1979. He got his first victory at Bristol in just his 16th start and had 11 top-five finishes that season. He was also named the Rookie of the Year. The following year, he beat veteran Cale Yarborough to win the Winston Cup Series. Dale thus became the first driver to win Rookie of the Year and the overall title in his first two seasons. It was just the start of an awesome career.

Earnhardt also won the championship in 1986, 1987, 1990,

1991, 1993, and 1994. His total of seven championships has been matched only by the great Richard Petty. His 76 race victories are among the most ever. His career **prize money** of more than $41 million was a record until Jeff Gordon overtook him in 2001.

Dale Earnhardt Sr. had learned racing from his father Ralph, a master of North Carolina's short tracks. So it was only natural that Dale would help his son learn about the world of racing. Dale Jr., a two-time Busch Series champion, joined the Winston Cup circuit in 2000.

Only a year later, however, tragedy struck the Earnhardt

A pair of aces: Dale and Dale Earnhardt Jr. celebrate a victory in an IROC race by Dale Sr.

family and NASCAR. On the last lap of the 2001 Daytona 500,

Dale Sr. was killed in a crash. Dale Jr. was in the race, too,

and cried with millions of others when he heard the news.

The younger Earnhardt faced the pressure of his father's

legacy well. Fans rallied to support him. Racers who had

battled with—and loved—his father helped him. Junior knew,

however, that once he got on the track, it was up to him. He

Dale Earnhardt had many great days on the track.
His 1998 victory in the Daytona 500 may have been
his greatest.

THE BODINES

NASCAR drivers Geoff, Brett, and Todd Bodine trace their racing roots to Chemung, New York. Their father and grandfather built a racetrack there when Geoff, the oldest brother, was just a year old.

From that beginning has come a solid family career. Between 1984 and 2001, no NASCAR race began without at least one Bodine on the track. The brothers have had many successes on the track. Geoff (right) was Rookie of the Year in 1982. He also won the 1986 Daytona 500.

Brett Bodine is unique in that he owns his own race car. He has competed in at least 29 races every year since joining Winston Cup full time in 1987. Ten years younger than Geoff, Brett's best finish was twelfth overall in 1990.

Todd, five years younger than Brett, began running Busch races in 1990. In 1993, he got his first taste of Winston Cup racing with 10 starts. Todd has earned a reputation as a strong relief driver in Winston Cup. He has had more success on the Busch circuit, where he finished second overall in 1997.

began to create his own memories with a great 2001 season. He finished in eighth place overall. Among his success were three race victories, 9 top-5 finishes, and 15 top-10s.

As long as there is NASCAR, the spirit of family racing will continue. From father to son, from brother to brother, the tradition is passed on. No matter what happens, the quest for speed continues.

Ahead of the pack just like his old man, Dale Earnhardt Jr. is racing ahead into the future.

THE BURTONS

As kids in South Boston, Virginia, Ward Burton and his brother Jeff raced go-karts. On weekends, the family traveled all over the state with their karts.

"I'm not sure how Mom and Dad put up with it," says Jeff. "I'm sure we fought the whole way there and the whole way back."

They kept up their battles on NASCAR tracks. In 1999, they were neck-and-neck to the end of the Las Vegas 400. Jeff finally won that race, one of his 17 career victories. He was also the 1994 Rookie of the Year and was third overall in 2000.

Ward, the older brother by six years, finished behind Jeff in the rookie voting. His first victory came in 1995. He finished 9th overall in the 1999 point standings and 10th overall in 2000.

The two Virginians had come a long way from go-karts. At least in NASCAR, they don't have to worry about fighting in the back seat.

Jeff and Ward Burton meet before a race. Ward made big news in 2002 with his victory in the Daytona 500.

GLOSSARY

go-karts—small, low, gas-powered vehicles often driven by youngsters; top speed of most karts is about 40 miles per hour. Races are held on twisty tracks with many turns.

legacy—the achievements and memories left behind by someone who has died

NASCAR—National Association for Stock Car Automobile Racing, the organizing group behind stock car racing

pit crew—the workers who work on a race car during a race; seven crew members can go onto a special area of the track to fuel the car and change tires, among other things

prize money—cash awarded to winners and others for doing well in races

relief driver—racer called in when a team's main driver is ill or injured

victory lap—after winning a race, victors drive alone around the track while fans cheer

Winston Cup—the series of races that determines the overall stock car champion; racers win points for victories, laps led, and other successes

FOR MORE INFORMATION ABOUT RACING FAMILIES

Books

Center, Bill. *Ultimate Stock Car*. New York: Dorling Kindersley, 2000.

Dale Earnhardt Jr.: Driving Force of a New Generation. Dallas: Beckett Publications, 2000.

Frankl, Ron. *Richard Petty*. Broomall, Penn: Chelsea House, 1996.

Persinger, Kathy. *Dale Earnhardt: The Intimidator*. Champaign, Ill.: Sports Publishing Inc., 2000.

Poole, David. *Dale Jarrett: Son of Thunder*. Champaign, Ill.: Sports Publishing, Inc., 2000.

Web Sites

The Official NASCAR Web Site
http://www.NASCAR.com
For an overview of an entire season of NASCAR as well as the history of the sport and a dictionary of racing terms

That's Racin'
http://www.Thatsracin.com
The *Charlotte* (North Carolina) *Observer* newspaper's site is great for fans who want to read about their favorite drivers.

Official Site of Petty Enterprises
http://www.pettyracing.com
The site contains the Petty's complete racing records. You can also see how Richard Petty's team's cars are doing in NASCAR races.

INDEX

ABOUT THE AUTHOR

Ted Brock has been writing books and articles about sports since 1972. He was a senior editor and staff writer with National Football League Properties and also taught sports writing at the University of Southern California. He has contributed to the *Los Angeles Times* and *USA Weekend*. He helped report on stock cars as the sports editor of the *Modesto* (California) *Bee*. He also helped produce Web sites for the 2000 Olympic Summer Games and 2002 Olympic Winter Games.